Contents

Introduction

Have you seen any good films at the cinema recently? Perhaps the one about dinosaurs brought back to life, or aliens trying to take over the galaxy? Even in the modern age of TVs and videos, there is nothing quite like an exciting film on the big screen, with glorious colour and all-round sound. Today, the motion picture business is a gigantic industry, spending and making billions each year, but its origins go back only a century.

The years from 1880 to 1910 were packed with scientific advances and inventions, from the motorcycle, motor car and aeroplane, to the electric light bulb and radio, and the discovery of **X-rays** and the structure of the atom. The arrival of the cinema was part of this busy, vital time. Like many other inventions, it was the result of numerous people making improvements and developments, and edging slowly forward.

The breakthrough came in a basement in Paris, in December 1895. On that cold winter night, brothers Auguste and Louis Lumière showed their first "moving pictures" to an open-mouthed audience. The Movie Age had begun.

An advertising poster from the late 1890s showing how audiences laughed at the first cinema joke, in the Lumières' Teasing the Gardener *(see page 25).*

Science Discoveries

THE

LUMIERE

BROTHERS

and the Cinema

Fabrice Calzettoni of The Lumière Institute
Edited and retold by
Steve Parker

Belitha Press

First published in Great Britain in 1995 by
Belitha Press Limited
31 Newington Green
London N16 9PU

Original text copyright © Institut Lumière 1994
This edition text copyright © Steve Parker 1995
Illustrations/photographs © in this format by
Belitha Press Limited 1995

ISBN 1 85561 382 4

Printed in China for Imago Publishing

British Library Cataloguing in Publication data for
this book is available from the British Library.

Photographic credits:
ET Archive: 6 top, 24 centre.
Mary Evans Picture Library: 8.
The Ronald Grant Archive: 26, 27.
Hulton Deutsch Collection: 7 bottom right,
    12/13 top.
Image Select/Ann Ronan Picture Library: 11 bottom,
    25 bottom.
The Lumière Institute, Lyon: title page, 4, 5 both,
    6 centre, 9, 11 top, 12 bottom, 13, 15, 16 right,
    17 left, 19, 22 bottom, 23, 24 top and bottom,
    25 top, 29.
Retrograph Archive: 7 bottom right ©Richard Balzer,
    22 top.
The Science Museum/Science and Society Picture
    Library: 7 centre and bottom left, 11 centre, 14 all,
    16 left, 17 right, 18.

Cover images provided by:
Mary Evans Picture Library; Hulton Deutsch
Collection; The Lumière Institute, Lyon; Ann Ronan
Picture Library.

Illustrations by Tony Smith
Diagrams by Peter Bull

Translator: Simona Sideri
Editor: Rachel Cooke
Design: Cooper Wilson Limited
Picture research: Juliet Duff
Consultant: David Robinson

Chapter One
The Early Years

In the nineteenth century, there was tremendous interest in the use of light, both in science and for entertainment. People loved the still pictures of magic lanterns (see panel) and the invention of photography had given them a whole new view of the world. People had also seen moving pictures on a small scale, in optical toys, such as the zoetrope (see page 7). The Lumière brothers were born into a world where scientists, doctors, inventors, photographers, magicians, and shadow-show producers were all searching for bigger and better ways to bring pictures to life, by making them move.

Auguste and Louis Lumière in a picture taken by their father in the late 1870s.

The magic lantern

Magic lanterns had been in existence since the 17th century. A bright light shone through a picture painted on glass, to "throw" or project its image on a white screen or wall. By changing the pictures quickly, and using mirrors, the images could be made to fade and reappear in a mysterious and magical way.

Magic lantern shows amazed and delighted the viewers. One very famous show was the *Phantasmagoria*, by Etienne-Gaspard Robertson. Shown in Paris from 1799, its ghosts and castles and villains terrified the audience, yet people came back again and again.

By the 19th century, factories were making thousands of magic lanterns, for use in public shows and in the home. They continued to be a great success, but soon faded away after the invention of the cinema.

The monsters of the Phantasmagoria *(left) were so frightening that viewers fainted, hid in terror, or even tried to fight them.*

The Swing *by Auguste Renoir (1892). A photograph would show this scene as it really appeared. Renoir has created an impression of beauty and mystery.*

Antoine Lumière taught, encouraged and later assisted his sons.

Persistence of vision

A motion picture or movie does not contain any moving pictures at all. It contains lots of stationary, still pictures. These are shown one after another, very quickly, 16 to 25 each second. The impression of movement is an optical illusion – a trick of the eye, relying on a feature known as **persistence of vision**.

Your eye takes a fraction of a second to respond to an image. It uses the light energy to make chemical changes in its delicate inner lining, the **retina**; it converts these into tiny electrical nerve signals; and it sends the signals to the brain.

When your brain receives the next set of nerve signals, from the next image, it joins the new picture onto the previous one. And so on, many times each second. Your eyes and brain "blur" or blend the many separate still pictures into a continuous scene.

Painters and photographers

The head of the Lumière family was the brothers' father Antoine Lumière. He was born in Ormoy, Haute-Saône, and became a portrait painter. From 1861 he lived with his wife Jeanne-Joséphine in Besançon, in Central France.

There were great changes in the world of art at this time. The recent invention of photography was being used to record people and objects and events. Painters, who had previously done this job, were now concentrating on less realistic styles which conveyed feelings, emotions, ideas and other abstract subjects.

The demand for portrait painters had declined and Antoine decided to take up a career in photography. He and his wife had a happy marriage and six children. The two eldest were Auguste, born on 24 October 1862, and Louis, born on 5 October 1864.

Spinning discs and wheels

Spinning discs and wheels

As the Lumière brothers grew up, they probably saw and played with common toys that showed "moving pictures"

• The spinning disc or thaumatrope was invented in about 1823. A card disc had a drawing of a cage on one side, and a bird on the other. Spin the disc fast using twisted strings, and the bird appears to be inside the cage. This illusion relied on our persistence of vision (see panel opposite)

• The phenakistoscope was devised in about 1833. A series of still pictures, each slightly different from the previous one, showing movement such as a person running, are arranged around the centre of a wheel. The wheel has slots in the edge. Spin the wheel, and look through the slots at the reflections in a mirror. Each slot reveals the picture beneath it for a fraction of a second, but persistence of vision means you see only one moving image.

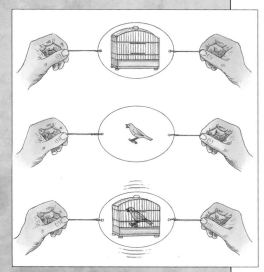

Thaumatrope

• The zoetrope was invented in 1833. A strip of pictures showing movement, as in the phenakisto-scope, is placed around the inside of a cylinder. This has slits in the side to look through. As the cylinder turns, you see the picture opposite through a slit for a fraction of a second, before it is replaced by the next slot and picture. Again, due to persistence of vision, you see an apparently moving picture.

Zoetrope

Phenakistoscope

A move to Lyon

In 1870 France went to war with Prussia. The enemy invaded as far as Dîjon, near Besançon and, to avoid the conflict, Antoine moved his whole family to Lyon, where he had an offer of work with the photographer Fatalot.

Antoine set up a studio in Rue de la Barre, calling himself a portrait photographer. He was able to make a good living, and his family continued to grow. Two daughters were born, Jeanne in 1870 and Juliette in 1873.

The Lumière studio continued to do well, and Antoine took on a number of employees. His two sons also did well at their junior schools. In 1877 the oldest, Auguste, passed the entrance exam to La Martinière Industrial School, to study science and technology.

The Franco-Prussian War in 1870 was short but bloody. Prussia's decisive victory led Napoleon III, then emperor of France, to fall from power. Since then France has remained a republic.

A time of change

Antoine Lumière in a publicity photograph for his own photographic studio in Lyon.

Both Auguste and Louis were excellent students throughout their school and college years. They studied a variety of sciences, including **optics** (the science of light), chemistry and physics. They found the work fairly easy, but they were rarely bored. They were always looking for new information and the latest knowledge and views.

The new technology that fascinated the brothers worried their father. Developments in photography meant that cameras and chemicals were becoming more available, and methods easier. It seemed as though photographers were setting up studios on almost every street corner. To make matters worse, George Eastman, an American, invented the small, hand-held camera, which allowed almost anyone to take a photograph.

Antoine realized that his business was in danger. He needed to change to survive.

Chapter Two

Better, Quicker Photographs

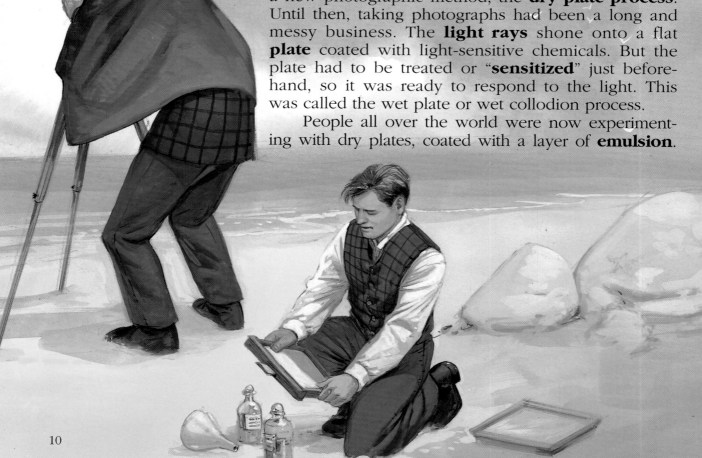

Auguste and Louis followed their father's interest in photography, and took and developed their own pictures, even on holiday. They used the wet plate process and had a small seaside cave as a darkroom.

In 1877, Auguste and Louis Lumière were on holiday in Saint-Enogat, in Brittany. Aged 15 and 13, they were already spending all their spare time on their favourite hobby – photography, using the **wet plate process** which was then popular. The brothers made a promise. They would stay together for ever, devoting their lives to photography and scientific research. Many young people make promises like this, but the Lumières kept theirs to the end of their lives.

Wet and dry

About this time, Antoine Lumière began to investigate a new photographic method, the **dry plate process**. Until then, taking photographs had been a long and messy business. The **light rays** shone onto a flat **plate** coated with light-sensitive chemicals. But the plate had to be treated or "**sensitized**" just beforehand, so it was ready to respond to the light. This was called the wet plate or wet collodion process.

People all over the world were now experimenting with dry plates, coated with a layer of **emulsion**.

Inventions in photography

The basic idea in photography is to shine light onto chemicals, and change the chemicals in some way, to produce a permanent picture or photographic image. Chemicals that contain silver are most popular. Photography has been invented in stages, and many different methods have come and gone in the past two centuries.

• The first permanent photographic images were made by Nicéphore Nièpce (1765-1833) around 1816-1828. He covered a pewter plate with a tar called "bitumen of Judea" which blackens and hardens when **exposed** to light. It took several hours to take each photograph. And the result was a **negative**, where light and dark are the reverse of real life. The lightest areas of the scene or object photographed appear darkest on the photograph, while the dark areas appear light.

• Louis Daguerre (1787-1851) made a **positive** image, where the light and dark areas are the right way round. His system of 1839 was called the daguerreotype, and used a silvered metal plate. It was a great success for a time. But no extra prints could be made from a daguerreotype. You had to take each photograph separately. Also each one needed to be exposed for several minutes. People's heads and bodies had to be clamped into stands, to stop them moving while the picture was being taken.

• William Fox Talbot (1800-1877) devised a system using paper covered in silver **salts**, during the 1830s. This produced a negative image. However a positive image could be made from the negative – and not only once, but many times. So you could make many positive copies from one negative, a method we still use today.

The first successful photograph, taken by Nièpce in 1826. It was taken over eight hours and shows the roofs and walls outside his upper-storey workroom.

(above) Fox Talbot's original camera and the lattice window he photographed at Lacock Abbey, England, in 1835.
(left) Mother and baby pose for a daguerreotype, heads clamped.

Eadweard Muybridge

Englishman Eadweard Muybridge (1830-1904) was a pioneer in photographing fast movements. He went to the USA, where he became a successful photographer. He also used the dry plate process to take many photographs in quick succession of moving animals and people, using rows of cameras. The results were a series of progressive photographs like those shown across these two pages. They could be viewed through a special lantern and appeared almost as moving pictures. But they were not, since they were not taken by one camera. Muybridge's books *Animal Locomotion* and *The Human Figure in Motion* were much admired.

Antoine Lumière and dog, photographed on an Etiquette Bleue dry plate. The short exposure time meant movement is "frozen" sharp, not blurred.

Emulsion was a jelly-like substance that would contain the light-sensitive chemicals and be ready to use, with no need for sensitizing immediately before use.

In 1878, as a result of the efforts of several people, the dry plate process became practical. The way was open for fast action photography, as explored by Muybridge (see panel).

Antoine Lumière wanted to improve the dry plate process. An emulsion which was even more sensitive to light could take photographs with exposures lasting only a tiny fraction of a second. He carried out many tests, but with limited success, as his methods were not very scientific or organized.

Auguste and Louis helped their father. They followed the scientific principles and methods they had learned at college. In 1881, Auguste was away doing his service in the army, but Louis carried on. He managed to develop a **gelatin** emulsion containing very light-sensitive, silver-based chemicals. This resulted in dry plates that they called Etiquette Bleue (Blue Label).

Back to success

The Lumières took over a warehouse in Lyon, at 25 Chemin Saint-Victor, Monplaisir. Antoine and Louis set up some equipment to make the dry plates. But money was short. Louis had only his 11-year-old sister to help him. When Auguste returned from the army, he found his family almost penniless.

Antoine was ready to give up, but Auguste refused to accept defeat. He and his father took charge of the photography studio, while Louis and his sister continued to make the plates. It was long, hard work, shut for hours in the photography darkrooms.

The Blue Label plates began to enjoy world-wide success and sales. The Lumières put the profits into more machines and paid people to make more plates. During this period Antoine and his wife had two more children, France in 1883 and Edouard in 1884.

By 1886 the family had made its fortune. The factory in Monplaisir was huge, and most of the people in the neighbourhood worked there. Auguste and Louis remembered their childhood promise, and used their profits for more photographic research.

Shooting birds with a photo-gun

In 1882, a Frenchman named Etienne-Jules Marey (1830-1904) invented a "photographic gun" with a rotating disc that took 12 pictures in one second. He wanted to use the pictures to study how birds fly. In 1888 he invented the chronophotographe. It used the newly available flexible paper roll film (see page 14), and took up to 40 photographs each second. But Marey was mainly interested in studying the individual photographs, and not in showing them to an audience. It was left to the Lumières and others to make the next set of advances.

Inside the first Lumière factory. The jars and bottles contain the chemicals which were mixed to make Etiquette Bleue dry plates.

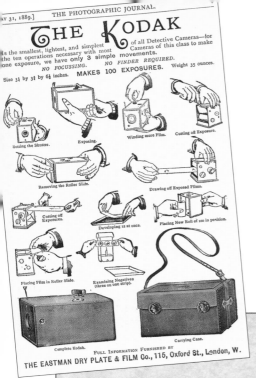

[AY 31, 1889.] THE PHOTOGRAPHIC JOURNAL.

THE KODAK

Is the smallest, lightest, and simplest of all Detective Cameras—for
the ten operations necessary with most Cameras of this class to make
one exposure, we have only 3 simple movements.
NO FOCUSSING. NO FINDER REQUIRED.
Size 3¼ by 3¾ by 6½ inches. MAKES 100 EXPOSURES. Weight 35 ounces.

Setting the Shutter. | Exposing. | Winding more Film. | Cutting off Exposure.

Removing the Roller Slide. | Drawing off Exposed Films.

Cutting off Exposures. | Developing 12 at once. | Placing New Roll of 100 in position.

Placing Film in Roller Slide. | Examining Negatives (three on one strip).

Complete Kodak. | Carrying Case.

FULL INFORMATION FURNISHED BY
THE EASTMAN DRY PLATE & FILM Co., 115, Oxford St., London, W.

Chapter Three
Making the First Movie

One day in the early 1890s, Antoine Lumière showed his sons a long strip or band of flexible photographic film, with holes punched along its sides. It was quite unlike the single flat, rigid photographic plates used in most cameras. It had been made by the US factory of George Eastman, for use in "peep-show" machines known as kinetoscopes (see panel). These had been invented by another American, Thomas Edison. The strip of film was very expensive. Antoine suggested that they try to produce a cheaper version.

George Eastman

American photographer and inventor George Eastman (1854-1932) improved the light-sensitive photographic emulsions of the dry plate process during the 1880s. In 1885 he devised a long strip of strong paper, coated with a layer of photographic emulsion and coiled into a roll. This could be wound through a camera, to take many photographs. Previously, a separate plate had to be put into the camera for each photograph, then taken out again.

In 1888, Eastman introduced a simple "box camera" that anyone could use – the first Kodak camera. It was supplied with a paper roll for 100 photographs. But the paper roll sometimes tore or wrinkled. So Eastman experimented with the use of **celluloid**, which was much stronger, and also see-through, for the type of photographs we call **transparencies**. Celluloid roll film was introduced in 1889.

The Eastman-Kodak Brownie (left) made photography cheap enough for the general public. Each contained a roll of celluloid film (above).

Pictures on a screen

In 1894, Auguste noticed a crowd of people outside a shop, waiting to look into one of the Edison kinetoscopes in Paris. He tried it for himself, and said that he was "charmed by the tiny animated images which paraded through the machine. I imagined how marvellous it would be if we were able to project these pictures on to a screen, to show them to a whole group of people at once. I decided to try to tackle this problem straightaway."

Auguste had decided that he wanted to show motion pictures on the big screen. To do this he needed four pieces of equipment:

1. A long strip or roll of photographic film, for the photos themselves.
2. A camera that would take photographs very quickly, at least 16 times each second.
3. A drive mechanism to pull the film through the camera, stopping it momentarily to allow each picture to be photographed.
4. A projector with a comparable mechanism, and the necessary lenses and light source to project the photographs on to a big screen, for many viewers.

The kinetoscope

On 9 May 1893, Thomas Edison (1847-1931) first launched the kinetoscope. Using Eastman's celluloid film, several short motion pictures were taken with his camera, the kinetograph, and then shown in a kinetoscope. This contained a loop of film 15 metres long, which played back the pictures at 40 per second. A rotating disc with a slot in it allowed a split-second flash of light to illuminate each **frame**. The viewer watched the "moving pictures" through a small hole at the top. The show lasted about 20 seconds.

The kinetoscope was a short-lived success. The quality of the pictures was poor, and only one person could view at a time. Edison was not interested in projecting pictures on to a big screen. He said: "Even if the whole world could watch animated photography at once, it still would not make money." For once, the great inventor was wrong.

Machines installed in the Kinetoscope Parlor on New York's Broadway in April 1894. Auguste Lumière first saw the kinetoscope in a similar parlour in Paris.

Celluloid film

The roll of film was already available – Eastman's celluloid film. It was strong, thin and transparent. It could be made in very long, narrow, flexible strips, coated with photographic emulsion and wound up into a roll. The many inventors working on moving pictures saw that celluloid film would be ideal for taking many photographs in quick succession.

Auguste tried for three months to find a satisfactory drive mechanism for use inside the camera or projector. The kinetoscope used film with holes punched along the side. The teeth of a **sprocket** fitted into the holes, and as the sprocket turned, it pulled the strip of film smoothly along. But the Lumières wanted the film to move along, stop while a photograph was taken or projected, then move on again, and so on, many times each second.

The Cinématographe

Louis Lumière was in bed recovering from influenza, when he told his brother that while he was ill, tossing and turning during a sleepless night, he had come up with a design for the drive mechanism (see page 18).

Using this idea, Louis worked on the camera for taking photographs, and the projector for showing them.

A series of successive pictures or frames from an 1896 Lumière film, representing about half a second of time. Note how the horses' legs move slightly in each frame; also note the sprocket holes along each edge.

Louis Lumière, in his old age, displays the inside of the original Cinématographe.

Reynaud's projector shone light through a long roll of painted images, via a mirror on to the back of the viewing screen. The cartoon actors were superimposed on a projected scene. But each "story strip", like the Light Pantomime (above), took hours to paint.

He was familiar with many existing "moving picture" machines, such as the praxinoscope (see panel). His design made the camera and projector the same machine – the **Cinématographe**. To make it work as a projector, a bright lamp was added, and used to shine light through the strip of film.

Louis prepared some design drawings, and the chief mechanic at the Monplaisir factory, Charles Moisson, built the first Cinématographe machine.

Shopping for celluloid

Louis had difficulty in obtaining Eastman's transparent celluloid film to use in his Cinématographe. His initial experiments – whose results he declared "excellent" – were on opaque photographic paper which could not be properly projected. Finally, he sent an employee to America to buy sheets of transparent celluloid, but without the light-sensitive coating. Back in Lyon, the Lumières coated the celluloid sheets with photographic emulsion, cut them into strips and punched the holes. They were ready to make the first motion picture.

An optical theatre

Emile Reynaud (1844-1918) invented the praxinoscope in 1877. It resembled the zoetrope (see page 7), but the centre of the cylinder had a series of flat mirrors. As these rotated, the viewer saw reflections of each picture from around the inner rim of the wheel, which the eye blurred into continuous movement.

Reynaud found a way of projecting the pictures onto a large screen. In his Optical Theatre, a series of pictures painted on to a long, flexible strip were reflected by the twirling mirrors on to a screen. These "moving pictures" lasted up to 15 minutes. But the pictures were drawings, not photographs and so not true cinema.

The Lumières' Cinématographe

The Cinématographe was both a camera and, when a lamp was attached, a projector, too. The individual photographs, or frames, were projected on to the screen at a rate of 16 per second. In fact, the speed varied from 12 to 24 frames per second, depending on how fast the operator turned the handle! (Later versions had clockwork and electric motors, and, by the 1920s, the rate of 24 frames per second became standard in the movie business.)

The drive mechanism was based on that which operated a sewing machine! A rotating

wheel called a **cam**, and a pair of wedges, made a set of small hooks or claws move. These claws fitted into the holes or perforations in the film, pulled it along, then withdrew. This left the film stationary as the claws moved back to the start of their cycle. While the film was stationary, the photograph could be taken or projected. (Photographs taken on moving film would be blurred.)

The drive mechanism was connected to a wheel with a large slot called a shutter. This turned around and allowed light to pass through at precisely the right time for each frame.

At this time the only film available was monochrome, which is black-and-white. Colour did not come into widespread use in the movies until the 1950s, though early films were sometimes coloured by hand.

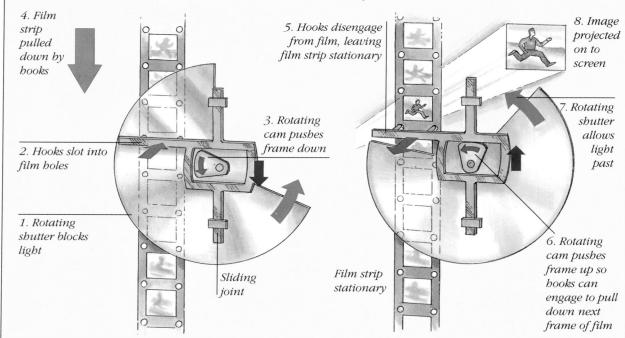

4. Film strip pulled down by hooks

5. Hooks disengage from film, leaving film strip stationary

8. Image projected on to screen

3. Rotating cam pushes frame down

2. Hooks slot into film holes

7. Rotating shutter allows light past

1. Rotating shutter blocks light

Sliding joint

Film strip stationary

6. Rotating cam pushes frame up so hooks can engage to pull down next frame of film

The first movie session

The Cinématographe was registered for an official **patent** in the name of both brothers, on 13 February 1895. On the morning of 19 March, Auguste and Louis waited near the gates of their factory in Monplaisir, Lyon. They had asked Monsieur Vernier, who lived directly opposite the factory gates, if they could place their Cinématographe machine behind the open window of his front room. It was a sunny day, but the street was quiet. Everyone was at work in the factory.

Louis checked that everything was ready. The celluloid photographic film was delicate, so even the temperature was important, 19°C in the shade. Finally, Louis' watch showed it was noon. The factory doors opened and the workers began to leave. Louis turned the handle of the Cinématographe. In less than a minute, everyone had gone and the doors closed again. The Lumières had taken the first motion picture in the history of cinema – *Leaving the Lumières' Factory* (*La sortie des usines Lumières*). It took just 50 seconds, and 800 frames (separate photographs).

A "still", or individual frame, from the Lumières' first movie – the factory gates open.

The Lumière brothers made the first movie in a room across the street from their factory. Louis turned the handle to work the drive mechanism and shutter of the Cinématographe.

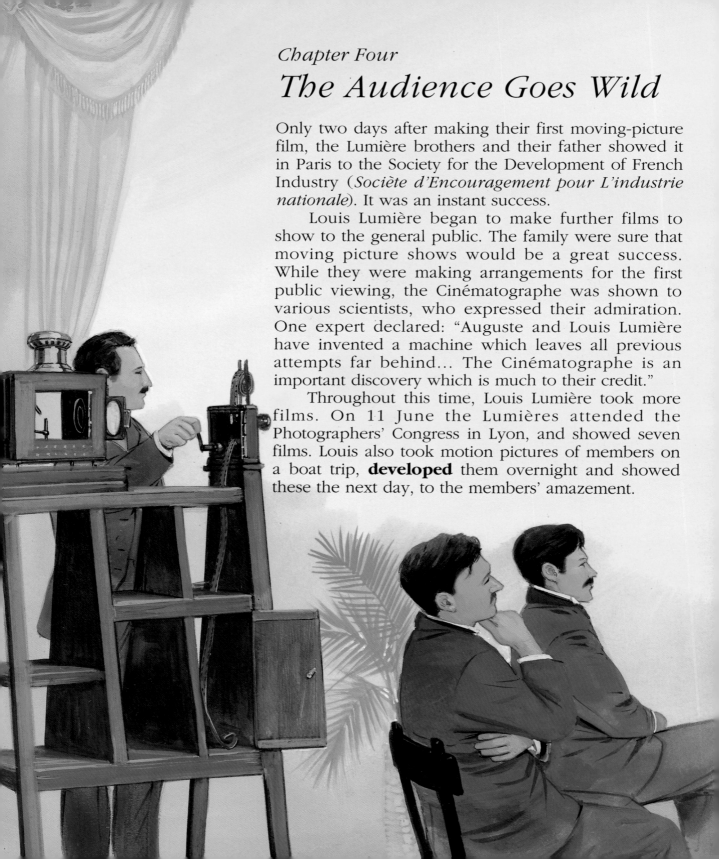

Chapter Four
The Audience Goes Wild

Only two days after making their first moving-picture film, the Lumière brothers and their father showed it in Paris to the Society for the Development of French Industry (*Sociète d'Encouragement pour L'industrie nationale*). It was an instant success.

Louis Lumière began to make further films to show to the general public. The family were sure that moving picture shows would be a great success. While they were making arrangements for the first public viewing, the Cinématographe was shown to various scientists, who expressed their admiration. One expert declared: "Auguste and Louis Lumière have invented a machine which leaves all previous attempts far behind... The Cinématographe is an important discovery which is much to their credit."

Throughout this time, Louis Lumière took more films. On 11 June the Lumières attended the Photographers' Congress in Lyon, and showed seven films. Louis also took motion pictures of members on a boat trip, **developed** them overnight and showed these the next day, to the members' amazement.

The first cinema

Antoine went to Paris to find a place for the first public show – the world's first cinema. Monsieur Volpini, owner of the Grand Café in Boulevard des Capucines, agreed to rent out an old billiard room in his basement. The business partner for the newly-formed company of Cinématographe Lumière, Clément Maurice, called it the Indian Room (*Salon Indien*).

Antoine and his sons proposed that the owners should have one-fifth of the money paid by any viewers. But this was refused. The owners wanted a daily payment of 30 francs, no matter how many people came. They were soon to regret this decision.

The first showing took place on 28 December 1895, at 9pm. Charles Moisson, who had made the machine, was chief mechanic and supervised the projection. Auguste and Louis were there. The admission price was one franc.

The Grand Café's basement billiard room was suitably dark for the first cinema. There were ten films shown that night, each about one minute long. Workers Leaving the Lumières' Factory and Teasing the Gardener were included in the programme.

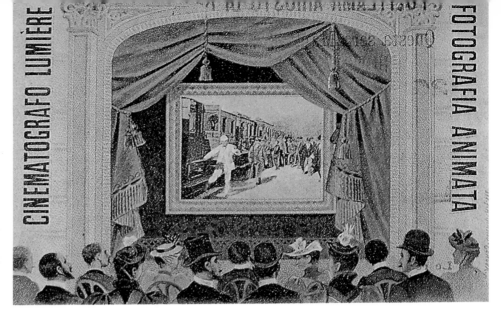

Posters advertising Lumière cinemas soon appeared in many cities, such as Genoa in Italy.

The first cinema show

Thirty-three curious people saw the first ever projection of a motion picture. Among them was Georges Méliès, a magician, conjuror and trick photographer, and friend of Antoine Lumière. He described the scene: "Together with the other guests I faced a small screen... After a moment a still image of Place Bellecour in Lyon appeared on the screen... I commented to my neighbour, 'Surely they haven't gathered us here to watch a [still] projection. I've been doing this sort of thing for at least 10 years.' I had just finished when a horse pulling a cart started moving towards us, followed by other vehicles, and some people... Soon the whole road had come to life. We were all stunned by the sight and sat there in amazement, our jaws hanging open."

Immediately the Lumières were offered huge sums of money – equivalent to thousands of pounds today. Several people wanted to buy their machine and the rights to make more of them. But the Lumières refused, saying that the Cinématographe might be an interesting scientific curiosity, but little else. In fact, it is more probable that the Lumières wanted to make money from their invention for themselves.

An entrance ticket to one of the early cinema shows, autographed by Louis Lumière himself.

Chapter Five
Cinema Around the World

The first night's takings at the Grand Café basement were 33 francs. Three weeks later, they were 2,000 francs per day. Thousands of people flocked to see the Cinématographe and left the show in wonder and astonishment. We are so used to cinema and television today, that it is difficult to imagine the enormous effect of the "living photographs" on people of the time.

Once the Cinématographes went on the market, the Lumières found it hard to keep up with the demand. About a hundred employees were trained to use them, and sent around the world to take films. The brothers went into partnership with the Planchon company, who made the celluloid film in France.

In February 1896 the Cinématographe opened in London. It soon reached New York, then Russia and China. The success was phenomenal.

Cashing in

The Lumière brothers had invented a simple drive mechanism for moving the film through the camera. Unlike Edison and others, they had

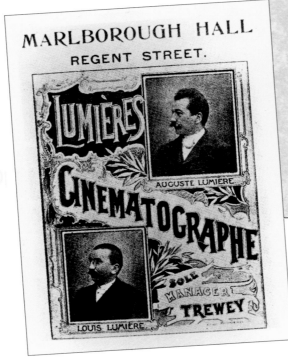

American cinema

In New York in April 1896, Thomas Edison launched his Vitascope projector, which enjoyed some success. The Lumières' Cinématographe arrived in June and began to gain ground. However in July 1897, the US government introduced new import laws which meant that people bringing Lumière Cinématographes and films into the country had to pay large sums of money, called import duties. The Lumière operators had their equipment taken away, and they were forced to flee New York.

More laws followed. It seemed as though the US government and US businesses wanted to drive out the cinema films and equipment of other countries. But the influence of the Lumières' invention was still enormous in America and contributed to the rapid development of American cinema technology.

The first London Cinématographe show opened in Regent Street on 20 February 1896. This is the cover of the programme.

The Lumière brothers together in their old age.

Colour photographs

In 1907 Louis invented the autochrome colour process, to make colour still photographs on glass plates, using a chemical based on potato starch. In the 1930s, faster and cheaper colour processes were devised by Agfa and Kodak, and these replaced autochrome. However, the autochrome process is still admired for its many and delicate colours, as this example shows.

Louis Lumière travelled widely and met many emerging cinema greats, such as animator Walt Disney (right).

realized that people liked to see motion pictures on a big screen. They also thought about what people wanted to watch: Louis wanted to make interesting films. He worked on ideas such as close-ups and camera angles.

However, other inventors and business people were not slow to copy or adapt the Lumières' ideas. By the end of the 19th century, the Lumières faced great competition, from people such as French industrial leader Charles Pathé (1863-1957). His film company was set up in 1896, and was the largest in the world from about 1900 to 1915.

Work must be fun

Louis decided to make work more fun again. In 1898 he invented a stereoscopic device, which made photographs appear **three-dimensional (3D)**, with "depth". In 1900, at a major exhibition, he projected a giant version of his film *Feeding the Baby*. The Monplaisir factory continued to operate, but the

The Lumières' films

The Lumières' list of films includes over 1600 titles. Their cameramen toured the world: they filmed the view from the Eiffel Tower in Paris, a Cinématographe show in London, Toledo Gate in Madrid, Venice's Grand Canal, a fire in Dublin, street life in Moscow, and Broadway in New York. They visited Japan, Saigon and Mexico, bringing these lands to audiences in Europe and North America. But best remembered are those early films made in France; they are rare glimpses into life at the end of the last century. A few are listed below:

Leaving the Lumières' Factory
La sortie des usines Lumières
The Lumière factory door opens and the workers emerge. There are three different versions, the earliest discovered only a few years ago.

The Cat's Meal
Le repas du chat
One of the Lumière children feeds a cat on a table. This was the first cinema close-up.

Teasing the Gardener
L'arroseur arrosé
A gardener waters his plants when a mischievous child stands on the hose pipe. The gardener looks into the end of the hose, the child lifts his foot, and *squirt*! This was the cinema's first make-believe story or fiction, rather than a scene from real life. It was also the first comedy!

Feeding the Baby
Le gouter du bébé
Auguste and his wife Marguerite feed their small baby Andrée. (Andrée died at the age of 24, throwing Auguste into despair.)

The Train Enters La Ciotat Station
Le train entrant en gare de La Ciotat
A train arrives and the passengers get off. When the enormous steam locomotive coming towards the camera was shown to the audience, it terrified them, and many people near the screen ran away in panic.

The Snowball Fight
La bataille de boule de neige
People in Monplaisir have a snowball battle, and a cyclist is bombarded from all sides. Using a variety of camera angles, Louis achieved a very artistic and evocative result.

Leaving the Lumières' Factory

Teasing the Gardener

Feeding the Baby

The Train Enters La Ciotat Station

brothers made no new films. In 1918, Louis sold the right to make the Cinématographe to Pathé. Auguste had followed an interest in medicine and his surgical inventions saved many lives.

The brothers spent their later years quietly and happily with their huge family at their house in La Ciotat, near Marseille. They kept their youthful pledge to carry on working and inventing together for the rest of their lives. Louis died in 1948, aged 84 years, and Auguste in 1954, aged 92. Their great legacy to motion pictures and the cinema lives on.

Louis Lumière is remembered on this commemorative medal which bears his likeness.

Film and video

When you watch a movie or other programme, it may not seem important whether it is on film or video. However the two technologies are totally different, even though the end result looks similar.

Film, a "visual medium", uses photographs – tiny see-through images of real scenes. It is designed mainly for projecting onto a big cinema screen.

Video is a "**magnetic-electronic** medium". The image exists as tiny patches of **magnetism** on the video tape. It is designed mainly for showing on a small television screen. Big video screens are available, but the picture quality is not generally as bright and clear as cinema. Special machinery can transfer film to video, or video to film. For home use, video has almost completely taken over from the film-based "home movies".

Director John Mackenzie discusses camera angles with the crew while filming The Fourth Protocol.

Chapter Six
After the Lumières

The Lumière brothers, and Louis in particular, made enormous contributions to the beginnings of cinema. The basic claw-like mechanism for pulling the film, that they invented and improved, is still used in cine cameras and projectors today. From the very beginning, the Lumières' Cinématographe system gave clear, sharp pictures. These were much better in quality than the rival systems of other inventors. The brothers put on the first ever cinema shows, and made a fascinating collection of early movie films.

However, almost as soon as cinema was invented, it changed with incredible speed and moved far beyond the Lumières' initial ideas. Movie-makers soon realized that to produce a good film, you needed not only good equipment but also good ideas for stories, an eye for action, another eye for beauty and so on. As technology advanced and movies became more ambitious so the jobs in the cinema business became more specialized and complicated. People became directors, producers, writers, film editors, camera operators, special effects experts, actors and actresses, and many others.

In the 1950s, 3D movies became popular. The audience had to wear spectacles with different coloured lenses to see the 3D effect. In the future, 3D effects may be far more dramatic – with no need for spectacles.

The first films were "silent". The only sounds were those made as the film was shown, usually musicians playing an accompaniment. In 1927 came the first "talkies", where the voices and other sounds were recorded at the same time as the pictures, and played back with them.

Colour cinema films became common in the 1950s. Then cinema technicians devised extra-wide curved screens for spectacular scenes, and very high quality stereo or quadraphonic sound. From the 1970s, computers were used to create ever more startling and realistic special effects.

Progress continues. The next generation of cinema-goers may watch a movie in full 3D. The actors will no longer be imprisoned on a flat screen. They will seem to walk out into the audience, so realistic that you could almost reach out and touch them.

Yet some of the cinema's most amazing moments were at its very beginning, and we owe them to the Lumières. The train coming into La Ciotat station made the audience scream with fear and run away in terror. Not many movies have that effect today.

Television and cinema

In the 1940s, people began to buy televisions for their homes. The pictures were sent in the form of **radio waves** through the air, detected by the aerial, and turned into images in the television set. The system was entirely electrical.

Immediately, cinema audiences began to fall. People preferred to sit at home in comfort, with the choice of several channels. But now cinema audiences are on the increase as people once again enjoy the spectacle and magic of "big screen" entertainment.

The World in the Lumières' Time

	1850–1875	**1876–1900**
Science	**1851** Hermann von Helmholtz invents the ophthalmoscope for looking into the inside of the eye **1862** Auguste Lumière is born **1864** Louis Lumière is born **1868** Thomas Edison invents his first device, to record votes in the US congress	**1877** Alexander Graham Bell and his colleagues found the Bell Telephone Company in the USA **1881** The first colour photograph is produced by Frederick Ives **1894** Guglielmo Marconi builds his first radio transmitter and receiver
Exploration	**1858** First telgraph lines laid across the Atlantic Ocean **1863** William Huggins shows the stars are made from elements also found on the Earth. Previously, it was thought that they were composed of substances not found on Earth	**1888** The National Geographic Society and its magazine are founded in the USA **1900** The ancient palace of Knossos, centre of the ancient Minoan civilization and home to the legendary Minotaur, is discovered on the island of Crete
Politics	**1852** New Zealand becomes largely self-governing **1861** The Boers set up a separate state in Transvaal, splitting from British-held South Africa **1870** The Franco-Prussian War begins	**1877** The first big industrial dispute occurs in the USA when the railway workers go on strike **1889** Portuguese control of Brazil ends as the country becomes a republic
Art	**1858** The first performance by the New York Philharmonic orchestra **1860** Charles Dickens publishes the novel *Great Expectations* **1860s** French painter Claude Monet begins his famous impressionist paintings	**1882** Robert Louis Stevenson publishes *Treasure Island* **1884** Peter Fabergé begins to make his famous gold-and-jewels Easter eggs for the Russian Tsar **1893** Engelbert Humperdinck writes his opera *Hansel and Gretel*

1901–1925

1910 Marie Curie publishes her *Treatise on Radioactivity*

1916 Research on preserving foods by freezing them is carried out by Clarence Birdseye

1924 Photographic images are sent by radio from New York to London

1902 A French expedition to Susa finds the Code of Hammurabi, the earliest known set of laws from Ancient Babylonia, engraved on a stone tablet

1912 Robert Scott and his party perish on their return journey from the South Pole

1902 Germany, Austria and Italy renew their Triple Alliance to 1914

1914 First World War begins. It ends in 1918

1919 The League of Nations is founded to promote world peace

1907 Pablo Picasso completes his painting *Les Demoiselles d'Avignon*, beginning the style of art called cubism

1915 D W Griffith's three-hour epic *The Birth of a Nation* sets new standards in all aspects of film-making

1926–1954

1935 A scale for measuring earthquakes is devised by Charles Richter

1940 The first colour television programmes are broadcast

1948 Louis Lumière dies

1954 Auguste Lumière dies

1926 An expedition to Mongolia's Gobi Desert discovers fossilized dinosaur eggs

1928 Roald Amundsen, first person to reach the South Pole, dies in a plane crash near Spitsbergen, while looking for shipwreck survivors

1929 The Vatican in Rome becomes independent of Italy and the world's smallest state

1939 Second World War begins. It ends in 1945

1953 Coronation of Queen Elizabeth II

1927 *The Jazz Singer* is the first "talking picture"

1938 *Snow White and the Seven Dwarfs* is the first full-length animated film

1929 Salvador Dali, leader of the surrealist movement, has his first exhibition of paintings

Glossary

cam: in mechanics, a part that goes around, or rotates, but not around its middle point, so that it is lop-sided or "off centre". It is used to change rotary (round and round) motion to oscillating (to and fro) motion.

celluloid: a flexible substance that is like plastic but is usually made in thin sheets or long, thin strips. It can be transparent or opaque, clear or coloured.

Cinématographe: the official name of the Lumières' first cinema device, which was both camera and projector. Later, it was sometimes used as a general name to describe other, similar devices.

develop: in photography, to treat a film which has been exposed to light with chemicals to reveal the picture or image on it.

dry plate process: a photographic process that does not use liquid chemicals for the original *plate* or film, but jelly-like or dry ones. This process largely replaced the earlier *wet plate process*.

emulsion: when one substance or chemical is spread out or "suspended" as tiny particles in another, as with the light-sensitive emulsion coating on photographic films or *plates*, or emulsion paint. It is usually thick or jelly-like.

exposed: in photography, when light is allowed to shine on the photographic film or *plate*, to affect the chemicals in the light-sensitive coating, so enabling a photograph to be taken.

frame: in cinema, a single one of the many pictures or images in the sequence that makes up a motion or moving picture.

gelatin: a jelly-like substance made from animal products such as bones, skins and cartilages (gristle). Used in photography, cooking, textiles and adhesives.

light rays: rays or waves of energy which we can see with our eyes. They are part of a whole range or spectrum of waves, called the electromagnetic spectrum, which includes *X-rays* and *radio waves*.

magnetic-electronic: involving both *magnetism* and electronics, which is the use of usually tiny amounts of electricity by transistors, silicon chips and similar devices.

magnetism: a still mysterious force, produced by a magnet or electric current, which can attract, repel or change objects and substances at a distance.

negative: in photography, a "reversed" picture or image, where the lightest parts of the scene or object photographed, such as the sun, are darkest, and the darker parts, such as shadows, are lighter. It is possible to print *positive* images from a translucent negative photograph.

optics: the scientific study of light.

plate: in photography, a flat, rigid object with a light-sensitive photographic coating or *emulsion*, as opposed to the same coating on flexible *celluloid* in the normal rolls of film.

patent: a legal document showing that someone is the official inventor of a device or product and has the sole right to make and sell it, for a time period. Others can do so only with permission of the patent holder. Patents are designed to stop other people "stealing" an invention on which someone has worked long and hard.

persistence of vision: an effect of the eyes and brain, in which we still "see" a scene for a split second after it has actually changed or disappeared. As a result, if we see more than 10-12 slightly different still or stationary scenes each second, then they tend to merge or blend into one continuous moving sequence.

positive: in photography, a "right way round" picture or image, which reproduces the light of the scene or object photographed as they appear to our eye. Positive film is used to produce *transparencies* and films for cinema projection.

radio waves: types of invisible waves used for conveying information in radio, television, radar and similar applications. They are part of a whole range or spectrum of waves, called the electromagnetic spectrum, which includes *light rays* and *X-rays*.

retina: the extremely thin, light-sensitive layer that lines the inside of the eye. It has more than 120 million microscopic units called cells, that convert the energy in *light rays* into tiny electrical nerve signals, which are sent to the brain.

salts: a group of chemicals, usually made by combining acids and alkalis. A familiar example is common table salt or "salt", sodium chloride. Silver-containing salts are used as the light-sensitive chemicals in photography.

sensitize: to make something sensitive, or ready to be changed, by a certain substance or effect, which previously would not have affected it.

sprocket: a wheel with relatively large teeth that usually project into holes in a chain or belt, like the "gear wheel" on a bicycle. When the sprocket turns, the chain or belt it is attached to will move as well.

three dimensional (3D): having height, breadth and depth, like objects in daily life. Objects on flat surfaces, like a painter's canvas or a photograph, exist only in two dimensions, height and breadth (width). The depth effect is an illusion.

transparencies: see-though (transparent) pictures or photographs. They are usually *positives* and are looked at by putting a light source behind them, in a viewer or using a projector and screen.

wet plate process: a photographic process that uses liquid chemicals for the original plate or film, rather than jelly-like or dry ones.

X-rays: invisible rays or waves of energy which can shine into and through soft substances, like skin and flesh, but not hard materials like bones or metals. This quality enables them to be used to look at our bones when covered by our skin.

X-rays are part of a whole range or spectrum of waves, called the electromagnetic spectrum, which includes *light rays* and *radio waves*.

Index